S0-AFE-586

THE ILLUSTRATED POETS

Oscar Wilde

EDITED BY
Daniel Burnstone

· PARRAGON ·

This is a Parragon Book.
Produced by Magpie Books,
an imprint of Robinson Publishing, London

Parragon
Unit 13-17, Avonbridge Trading Estate,
Atlantic Road, Avonmouth,
Bristol, BS11 9QD

Reprinted 1996

This book is sold subject to the condition that it shall not,
by way of trade or otherwise, be lent, resold, hired out or
otherwise circulated without the publisher's prior consent
in any form of binding or cover than that in which it is
published and without similar condition being imposed on
the subsequent purchaser.

Collection copyright © Parragon Book Service Ltd 1994

Cover picture: Oscar Wilde, 1882, by Napoleon Sarony,
The National Portrait Gallery, London. Illustrations
courtesy of: Christies Images; Mary Evans Picture Library.

ISBN 0 75250 041 4

A copy of the British Library Cataloguing in Publication
Data is available from the British Library.

Typeset by Hewer Text Composition Services, Edinburgh
Printed in Singapore by Tien Wah Press

Contents

❧ ART ❧

'A poem is well written or badly written. In art there should be no reference to a standard of good or evil. The presence of such a reference implies incompleteness of vision. The Greeks understood this principle, and with perfect serenity enjoyed works of art that, I suppose, some of my critics would never allow their families to look at. The enjoyment of poetry does not come from the subject, but from the language and rhythm. Art must be loved for its own sake, and not criticised by a standard of morality.'

In Interview

Art never expresses anything but itself. It has an independent life, just as Thought has, and develops purely on its own lines. It is not necessarily realistic in an age of realism, nor spiritual in an age of faith. So far from being the creation of its time, it is usually in direct opposition to it, and the only history it preserves for us is the history of its own progress.

The Decay of Lying

All bad art comes from returning to Life and Nature, and elevating them to ideals. Life and Nature may sometimes be used as part of Art's rough material, before they are of any real service to Art they must be translated into artistic conventions. The moment Art surrenders its imaginative medium it surrenders everything. As a method Realism is a complete failure, and the two things that every artist should avoid are modernity of form and modernity of subject matter.

The Decay of Lying

There are two ways of disliking art . . . One is to dislike it. The other is to like it rationally.

The Critic as Artist.

An age that has no criticism is either an age in which art is immobile, hieratic, and confined to the reproduction of formal types, or an age that possesses no art at all.

The Critic as Artist.

Art finds her own perfection within, and not outside of, herself. She is not to be judged by any external standards of resemblance. She is a veil, rather than a mirror. She has flowers that no forests know of, birds that no woodland possesses. She makes and unmakes many worlds, and can draw the moon from heaven with a scarlet thread. Hers are the forms more real than living man, and hers the great archetypes of which things that have existence are but unfinished copies. Nature has, in her eyes, no law, no uniformity.

The Decay of Lying

We try to improve the conditions of the race by means of good air, free sunlight, wholesome water, and hideous bare buildings for the better housing of the lower orders. But these things merely produce health, they do not produce beauty. For this, Art is required, and the true disciples of the great artist are not his studio-imitators, but those who become like his work of art, be they plastic as in Greek days, or pictorial as in modern times; in a word, Life is Art's best, Art's only pupil.

The Decay of Lying

Things are because we see them, and what we see, and how we see it depends on the Arts that have influenced us. At present, people see fogs, not because there are fogs, but because poets and painters have taught them the mysterious loveliness of such effects. There may have been fogs for centuries in London. I dare say there were. But no one saw them, and so we do not know anything about them. They did not exist till Art had invented them. Now, it must be admitted, fogs are carried to excess. They have become the mere mannerism of a clique, and the exaggerated realism of their method gives dull people bronchitis. Where the cultured catch an effect, the uncultured catch cold.

The Decay of Lying.

Nobody of any real culture ever talks about the beauty of a sunset. Sunsets are quite old-fashioned. They belong to the time when Turner was the last note in art. To admire them is a distinct sign of provincialism. Upon the other hand they go on. Yesterday evening Mrs. Arundel insisted on my going to the window and looking at the glorious sky, as she called it. Of course I had to look at it. She is one of those absurdly pretty Philistines, to whom one can deny nothing. And what was it? It was simply a very second-rate Turner, a Turner of bad period, with all the painter's worst faults exaggerated and over-emphasized.

The Decay of Lying.

No great artist ever sees things as they really are. If he did he would cease to be an artist.

The Decay of Lying.

Paradox though it may seem — and paradoxes are always dangerous things — it is none the less true that life imitates art far more than art imitates life.

The Decay of Lying.

Mediocrity weighing mediocrity in the balance, and incompetence applauding its brother — that is the spectacle which the artistic activity of England affords us from time to time.

The Critic as Artist.

Modern pictures are, no doubt, delightful to look at. At least, some of them are. But they are quite impossible to live with; they are too clever, too assertive, too intellectual. Their meaning is too obvious, and their method too clearly defined. One exhausts what they have to say in a very short time, and then they become as tedious as one's relations.

The Critic as Artist.

W e can forgive a man for making a useful thing as long as he does not admire it. The only excuse for making a useless thing is that one admires it intensely. All art is quite useless.

The Picture of Dorian Gray.

Art is the most intense mode of Individualism that the world has known.

The Soul of Man Under Socialism.

f or a man to be a dramatic critic is as foolish and as inartistic as it would be for a man to be a critic of epics or a pastoral critic, or a critic of lyrics. All modes of art are one, and the modes of the art that employs words as its medium are quite indivisible. The result of the vulgar specialization of criticism is an elaborate scientific knowledge of the stage — almost as elaborate as that of the stage-carpenter and quite on a par with that of the call-boy — combined with an entire incapacity to realize that a play is a work of art, or to receive any artistic impressions at all.'

In Conversation

'Poets, you know, are always ahead of science; all the great discoveries of science have been stated before in poetry. So far as science comes in contact with our school, we love its practical side; but we think it absurd to seek to make the material include the spiritual, to make the body mean the soul, to say that one emotion is only a secretion of sugar, and another nothing but a contraction of the spine.'

In Interview

All art is immoral. For emotion for the sake of emotion is the aim of art, and emotion for the sake of action is the aim of life.

The Critic as Artist.

The aesthete

. . . **t**he more we study Art, the less we care for Nature. What Art really reveals to us is Nature's lack of design, her curious crudities, her extraordinary monotony, her absolutely unfinished condition. Nature has good intentions, of course, but, as Aristotle once said, she cannot carry them out.

The Decay of Lying.

🙬 SOCIETY 🙮

What is interesting about people in good society is the mask that each one of them wears, not the reality that lies behind the mask.

The Decay of Lying.

If one could only teach the English how to talk, and the Irish how to listen, society here would be quite civilised.

An Ideal Husband.

It is only by not paying one's bills that one can hope to live in the memory of the commercial classes.

Phrases and Philosophies for the Use of the Young.

I love London Society! I think it has immensely improved. It is entirely composed now of beautiful idiots and brilliant lunatics. Just what Society should be.

An Ideal Husband.

There is something tragic about the enormous number of young men there are in England at the present moment who start life with perfect profiles, and end by adopting some useful profession.

Phrases and Philosophies for the Use of the Young.

The chief advantage that would result from the establishment of Socialism is, undoubtedly, the fact that Socialism would relieve us from that sordid necessity of living for others which, in the present condition of things, presses so hardly upon almost everybody. In fact, scarcely any one at all escapes.
The Soul of Man Under Socialism.

Cultivated leisure is the aim of man.
The Soul of Man Under Socialism.

. . . the more we study Art, the less we care
for Nature.

T he majority of people spoil their lives by an unhealthy and exaggerated altruism – are forced, indeed so to spoil them. They find themselves surrounded by hideous poverty, by hideous ugliness, by hideous starvation. It is inevitable that they should be strongly moved by all this. The emotions of man are stirred more quickly than man's intelligence; and as I pointed out some time ago in an article on the function of criticism, it is much more easy to have sympathy with suffering than it is to have sympathy with thought. Accordingly, with admirable, though misdirected intentions, they very seriously and very sentimentally set themselves to the task of remedying the evils that they see. But their remedies do not cure the disease: they merely prolong it. Indeed, their remedies are part of the disease.

They try to solve the problem of poverty,

for instance, by keeping the poor alive; or, in the case of a very advanced school, by amusing the poor.

But this is not a solution; it is an aggravation of the difficulty. The proper aim is to try and reconstruct society on such a basis that poverty will be impossible. And the altruistic virtues have really prevented the carrying out of this aim.

The Soul of Man Under Socialism

The Art Class, Edouard Hamman

W e live in the age of the overworked, and the under-educated; the age in which people are so industrious that they become absolutely stupid.

The Critic as Artist.

Each class preaches the importance of those virtues it need not exercise. The rich harp on the value of thrift, the idle grow eloquent over the dignity of labour.

In Conversation.

N ever speak disrespectfully of society.
Only people who can't get into it do
that.

In Conversation.

Work is the curse of the drinking classes.

In Conversation.

Society, civilized society at least, is never
very ready to believe anything to the detriment of those who are both rich and
fascinating.

The Picture of Dorian Gray.

E verybody one meets is a paradox nowadays. It is a great bore. It makes society
so obvious.

An Ideal Husband.

It is very vulgar to talk about one's business.
Only people like stockbrokers do that, and
then merely at dinner-parties.

The Importance of Being Earnest.

A child can understand a punishment
inflicted by an individual, such as a
parent or guardian, and bear it with a certain
amount of acquiesence. What it cannot
understand is a punishment inflicted by
society.

Letter to the Daily Chronicle.

Society often forgives the criminal; it never
forgives the dreamer.

The Critic as Artist.

Cultivated leisure is the aim of man.

❧ LOVE ❧

Love is an illusion.
The Picture of Dorian Gray.

What a silly thing love is! It is not half as useful as logic, for it does not prove anything and it is always telling one things that are not going to happen, and making one believe things that are not true.
The Nightingale and the Rose.

Always! That is a dreadful word. It makes me shudder when I hear it. Women are so fond of using it. They spoil every romance by trying to make it last for ever. It is a meaningless word too. The only difference between a caprice and a lifelong passion is that the caprice lasts a little longer.

The Picture of Dorian Gray.

Lady Windermere's Fan

I might mimic a passion that I do not feel, but I cannot mimic one that burns one like fire.

The Picture of Dorian Gray.

Between men and women there is no friendship possible. There is passion, enmity, worship, love, but no friendship.

Lady Windermere's Fan.

Young men want to be faithful and are not; old men want to be faithless and cannot.

The Picture of Dorian Gray.

The very essence of romance is uncertainty. If ever I get married, I'll certainly try to forget the fact.

The Importance of Being Earnest.

Those who are faithful know only the trivial side of love: it is the faithless who know love's tragedies.

The Picture of Dorian Gray.

Romance should never begin with sentiment. It should begin with science and end with a settlement.

An Ideal Husband.

a really *grande passion* is comparatively rare nowadays. It is the privilege of people who have nothing to do. That is the one use of the idle classes in a country.

A Woman of No Importance.

. . . not love at first sight, but love at the end of the season, which is so much more satisfactory.

Lady Windermere's Fan.

The worst of having a romance of any kind is that it leaves one so unromantic.

The Picture of Dorian Gray.

There is always something ridiculous about the emotions of people whom one has ceased to love.

The Picture of Dorian Gray.

MRS. ALLONBY: There is a beautiful moon tonight.

LORD ILLINGWORTH: Let us go and look at it. To look at anything that is inconstant is charming nowadays.

A Woman of No Importance.

Afternoon Tea, Harold Knight

PRINCE PAUL: . . . You want a new excitement, Prince. Let me see – you have been married twice already suppose you try – falling in love for once.

Vera, or The Nihilists.

To love oneself is the beginning of a life-long romance.
Phrases and Philosophies for the Use of the Young.

A kiss may ruin a human life.
A Woman of No Importance.

Yet each man kills the thing he loves,
   By each let this be heard,
Some do it with a bitter look,
   Some with a flattering word.
The coward does it with a kiss,
   The brave man with a sword!

Some kill their love when they are young,
   And some when they are old;
Some strangle with the hands of Lust,
   Some with the hands of Gold:
The kindest use a knife, because
   The dead so soon grow cold.

A Woman of no Importance

Some love too little, some too long,
    Some sell, and others buy;
Some do the deed with many tears,
    And some without a sigh:
For each man kills the thing he loves,
    Yet each man does not die.

He does not die a death of shame
    On a day of dark disgrace,
Nor have a noose about his neck,
    Nor a cloth upon his face,
Nor drop feet foremost through the floor
    Into an empty space.

He does not sit with silent men
  Who watch him night and day;
Who watch him when he tries to weep,
  And when he tries to pray;
Who watch him lest himself should rob
  The prison of its prey.

He does not wake at dawn to see
  Dread figures throng his room,
The shivering Chaplain robed in white,
  The Sheriff stern with gloom,
And the Governor all in shiny black,
  With the yellow face of Doom.

He does not rise in piteous haste
    To put on convict-clothes,
While some coarse-mouthed Doctor gloats,
and notes
    Each new and nerve-twitched pose,
Fingering a watch whose little ticks
    Are like horrible hammer-blows.

He does not feel that sickening thirst
    That sands one's throat, before
The hangman with his gardener's gloves
    Comes through the padded door,
And binds one with three leathern thongs,
    That the throat may thirst no more.

He does not bend his head to hear
    The Burial Office read,
Nor, while the anguish of his soul
    Tells him he is not dead,
Cross his own coffin, as he moves
    Into the hideous shed.

He does not stare upon the air
    Through a little roof of glass:
He does not pray with lips of clay
    For his agony to pass;
Nor feel upon his shuddering cheek
    The kiss of Caiaphas.

★ ★ ★

Venus and Cupid, Walter Crane

In Reading gaol by Reading town
　　There is a pit of shame,
And in it lies a wretched man
　　Eaten by teeth of flame,
In a burning winding-sheet he lies,
　　And his grave has got no name.

And there, till Christ call forth the dead,
　　In silence let him lie:
No need to waste the foolish tear,
　　Or heave the windy sigh:
The man had killed the thing he loved,
　　And so he had to die.

And all men kill the thing they love,
    By all let this be heard,
Some do it with a bitter look,
    Some with a flattering word,
The coward does it with a kiss,
    The brave man with a sword!
        From *The Ballard of Reading Gaol*

Iseult, Aubrey Beardsley

❧ MORALITY AND TRUTH ❧

G ood resolutions are useless attempts to interfere with scientific laws. Their origin is pure vanity. Their result is absolutely nil. They give us, now and then, some of those luxurious sterile emotions that have a certain charm for the weak. That is all that can be said of them. They are simply cheques that men draw on a bank where they have no account.

The Picture of Dorian Gray.

Many a young man starts in life with a natural gift for exaggeration which, if nurtured in congenial and sympathetic surroundings, or by the imitation of the best models, might grow into something really great and wonderful. But, as a rule, he comes to nothing. He either falls into careless habits of accuracy, or takes to frequenting the society of the aged and well-informed.

Both things are equally fatal to his imagination, as indeed they would be to the imagination of anybody, and in a short time he develops a morbid and unhealthy faculty of truth-telling, begins to verify all statements made in his presence, has no hesitation in contradicting people who are much younger than himself, and often ends by writing novels which are so life-like that no one can possibly believe in their probability.

The Decay of Lying

C onscience and cowardice are really the same things. Conscience is the trade-name of the firm.

The Picture of Dorian Gray.

It is a terrible thing for a man to find out suddenly that all his life he has been speaking nothing but the truth.

The Importance of Being Earnest.

To be either a Puritan, a prig or a preacher is a bad thing. To be all three at once reminds me of the worst excesses of the French Revolution.

Letter from Paris, June 1898.

Bacchus and Ceres, Hans von Aachen

. . . **d**uty is what one expects from others, it is not what one does oneself.

A Woman of No Importance

Moderation is a fatal thing. Enough is as bad as a meal. More than enough is as good as a feast.

The Picture of Dorian Gray.

To be good is to be in harmony with oneself. Discord is to be forced to be in harmony with others.

In Conversation.

There is no such thing as a good influence. All influence is immoral — immoral from the scientific point of view.

The Picture of Dorian Gray.

The truth is rarely pure and never simple. Modern life would be very tedious if it were either, and modern literature a complete impossibility.

The Importance of Being Earnest.

A cynic is a man who knows the price of everything and the value of nothing.

Lady Windermere's Fan.

The first duty in life is to be as artificial as possible.

S everal plays have been written lately that deal with the monstrous injustice of the social code of morality at the present time. It is indeed a burning shame that there should be one law for men and another law for women. I think there should be no law for anybody.

In an Interview.

There is no such thing as a moral or an immoral book. Books are well written, or badly written. That is all.

No artist has ethical sympathies. An ethical sympathy in an artist is an unpardonable mannerism of style.

The Picture of Dorian Gray (The Preface)

What people call insincerity is simply a method by which we can multiply our personalities.

The Critic as Artist.

A ny preoccupation with ideas of what is right or wrong in conduct shows an arrested intellectual development.
Phrases and Philosophies for the Use of the Young.

Nothing that actually occurs is of the smallest importance.
Phrases and Philosophies for the Use of the Young.

In all unimportant matters, style, not sincerity, is the essential. In all important matters, style, not sincerity, is the essential.
Phrases and Philosophies for the Use of the Young.

To be good, according to the vulgar standard of goodness, is obviously quite easy. It merely requires a certain amount of sordid terror, a certain lack of imaginative thought, and a certain low passion for middle-class respectability.

The Critic as Artist.

A little sincerity is a dangerous thing, and a great deal of it is absolutely fatal.

The Critic as Artist.

Salomé

A truth ceases to be true when more than one person believes in it.
Phrases and Philosophies for the Use of the Young.

Modern morality consists in accepting the standard of one's age. I consider that for any man of culture to accept the standard of his age is a form of the grossest immorality.
The Picture of Dorian Gray.

Wickedness is a myth invented by good people to account for the curious attractiveness of others.

Phrases and Philosophies
for the Use of the Young.

The first duty in life is to be as artificial as possible. What the second duty is no one has yet discovered.

Phrases and Philosophies
for the Use of the Young.

If one tells the truth, one is sure, sooner or later, to be found out.

Phrases and Philosophies
for the Use of the Young.

In the Row, out of Season, Rose Barton

M orality is simply the attitude we adopt
to people whom we personally dislike.

An Ideal Husband.

If you pretend to be good, the world takes
you very seriously. If you pretend to be bad,
it doesn't. Such is the astounding stupidity of
optimism.

Lady Windermere's Fan.

M oderation is a fatal thing. Nothing succeeds like excess.

A Woman of No Importance.

If we lived long enough to see the results of our actions it may be that those who call themselves good would be sickened with a dull remorse, and those whom the world calls evil stirred by a noble joy.

The Critic as Artist.

M orality does not help me. I am a born antinomian. I am one of those who are made for exceptions, not for laws. But while I see that there is nothing wrong in what one does, I see that there is something wrong in what one becomes. It is well to have learned that.

De Profundis

❧ IMPRESSIONS ❧

Les Silhouettes

The sea is flecked with bars of grey,
The dull dead wind is out of tune,
And like a withered leaf the moon
Is blown across the stormy bay.

Etched clear upon the pallid sand
The black boat lies: a sailor boy
Clambers aboard in careless joy
With laughing face and gleaming hand.

And overhead the curlews cry,
Where through the dusky upland grass
The young brown-throated reapers pass,
Like silhouettes against the sky.

The sky is laced with fitful red,
The circling mists and shadows flee

La Fuite de la Lune

To outer senses there is peace,
A dreamy peace on either hand,
Deep silence in the shadowy land,
Deep silence where the shadows cease.

Save for a cry that echoes shrill
From some lone bird disconsolate;
A corncrake calling to its mate;
The answer from the misty hill.

And suddenly the moon withdraws
Her sickle from the lightening skies,
And to her sombre cavern flies,
Wrapped in a veil of yellow gauze.

Le Réveillon

The sky is laced with fitful red,
  The circling mists and shadows flee,
  The dawn is rising from the sea,
Like a white lady from her bed.

And jagged brazen arrows fall
  Athwart the feathers of the night,
  And a long wave of yellow light
Breaks silently on tower and hall,

And spreading wide across the wold,
  Wakes into flight some fluttering bird,
  And all the chestnut tops are stirred,
And all the branches streaked with gold.

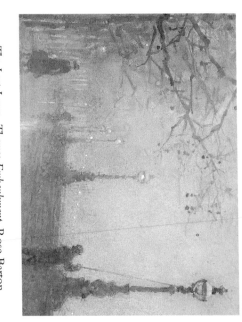

The Last Lamp, Thames Embankment, Rose Barton

After the first glass of absinthe you see things as you wish they were. After the second you see them as they are not. Finally you see things as they really are, and that is the most horrible thing in the world. I mean disassociated. Take a top hat. You think you see it as it really is. But you don't because you associate it with other things and ideas. If you had never heard of one before, and suddenly saw it alone, you'd be frightened or you'd laugh. That is the effect absinthe has, and that is why it drives men mad. Three nights I sat up all night drinking absinthe, and thinking that I was singularly clear-headed and sane. The waiter came in and began watering the saw-dust. The most wonderful flowers, tulips, lilies and roses, sprang up, and made a garden in the café 'Don't you see them?' I said to him. '*Mais non, monsieur, il n'y a rien.*'

In Conversation.

Les Ballons

Against these turbid turquoise skies
   The light and luminous balloons
   Dip and drift like satin moons,
Drift like silken butterflies;

Reel with every windy gust,
   Rise and reel like dancing girls,
   Float like strange transparent pearls,
Fall and float like silver dust.

Now to the low leaves they cling,
   Each with coy fantastic pose,
   Each a petal of a rose
Straining at a gossamer string.

Then to the tall trees they climb,
   Like thin globes of amethyst,
   Wandering opals keeping tryst
With the rubies of the lime.

Symphony in Yellow

An omnibus across the bridge
   Crawls like a yellow butterfly,
    And, here and there, a passer-by
Shows like a little restless midge.

Big barges full of yellow hay
   Are moved against the shadowy wharf,
    And, like a yellow silken scarf,
The thick fog hangs along the quay.

The yellow leaves begin to fade
   And flutter from the Temple elms,
    And at my feet the pale green Thames
Lies like a rod of rippled jade.

The Sphinx

In a dim corner of my room for longer than
my fancy thinks
A beautiful and silent Sphinx has watched
me through the shifting gloom.

Inviolate and immobile she does not rise she
does not stir
For silver moons are naught to her and
naught to her the suns that reel.

Portrait of Oscar Wilde by Oliver Plaque

Red follows grey across the air, the waves of
moon-light ebb and flow
But with the Dawn she does not go and in
the night-time she is there.

Dawn follows Dawn and Nights grow old
and all the while this curious cat
Lies couching on the Chinese mat with eyes
of satin rimmed with gold.

Upon the mat she lies and leers and on the
tawny throat of her
Flutters the soft and silky fur or ripples to her
pointed ears.

Come forth, my lovely seneschal! so som-
nolent, so statuesque!
Come forth you exquisite grotesque! half
woman and half animal!

Come forth my lovely languorous Sphinx!
and put your head upon my knee!
And let me stroke your throat and see your
body spotted like the Lynx!

And let me touch those curving claws of
yellow ivory and grasp
The tail that like a monstrous Asp coils round
your heavy velvet paws!

I 'll be a poet, a writer, a dramatist, somehow or other I'll be famous, and if not famous I'll be notorious. Or perhaps . . . I'll rest and do nothing . . . These things are on the knees of the Gods. What will be, will be.
In Conversation at Oxford.

We watch ourselves, and the mere wonder of the spectacle enthralls us, and I am the only person in the world I should like to know thoroughly, but I don't see any chance of it just at present.

In Conversation.

I t is sad. One half of the world does not believe in God, and the other half does not believe in me.

In Conversation.

The only writers who have influenced me are Keats, Flaubert and Walter Pater, and before I came across them I had already gone more than half-way to meet them.

In Conversation.

'The first time that the absolute stupidity of the English people was ever revealed to me was one Sunday at the University Church, when the preacher opened his sermon in something this way: "When a young man says not in polished banter, but in sober earnestness, that he finds it difficult to live up to the level of his blue china, there has crept into these cloistered shades a form of heathenism which it is our bounden duty to fight against and crush out, if possible." I need hardly say that we were delighted and amused at the typical English way in which our ideas were misunderstood. They took our epigrams as earnest, and our paradoxes as prose.

In Interview

My name has two 'O's, two 'F's and two 'W's. A name which is destined to be in everybody's mouth must not be too long. It comes so expensive in the advertisements. When one is unknown, a number of Christian names are useful, perhaps needful. As one becomes famous, one sheds some of them, just as a balloonist, when rising higher, sheds unnecessary ballast . . . All but two of my five names have already been thrown overboard. Soon I shall discard another and be known simply as 'The Wilde' or 'The Oscar'.

In Conversation.

I was a man who stood in symbolic relations to the art and culture of my age. I had realised this for myself at the very dawn of my manhood, and had forced my age to realise it afterwards. Few men hold such a position in their own lifetime, and have it so acknowledged. It is usually discerned, if discerned at all, by the historian, or the critic, long after both the man and his age have passed away. With me it was different. I felt it myself, and made others feel it. Byron was a symbolic figure, but his relations were to the passion of his age and its weariness of passion. Mine were to something more noble, more permanent, of more vital issue, of larger scope.

De Profundis.

P raise makes me humble, but when I am abused I know I have touched the stars.
In Conversation.

I must say to myself that I ruined myself, and that nobody great or small can be ruined except by his own hand. I am quite ready to say so. I am trying to say so, though they may not think it at the present moment. This pitiless indictment I bring without pity against myself. Terrible as was what the world did to me, what I did to myself was far more terrible still.

De Profundis

Tired of being on the heights, I deliberately went to the depths in the search for new sensation. What the paradox was to me in the sphere of thought, perversity became to me in the sphere of passion. Desire, at the end, was a malady, or a madness, or both. I grew careless of the lives of others. I took pleasure where it pleased me, and passed on. I forgot that every little action of the common day makes or unmakes character, and that therefore what one has done in the secret chamber one has some day to cry aloud on the housetop.

De Profundis

I treated art as the supreme reality and life as a mere mode of fiction. I awoke the imagination of my century so that it created myth and legend around me. I summed up all systems in a phrase and all existence in an epigram. . . .

But I let myself be lured into long spells of senseless and sensual ease. I amused myself with being a *flâneur*, a dandy, a man of fashion. I surrounded myself with the smaller natures and the meaner minds. I became the spendthrift of my own genius and to waste an eternal youth gave me a curious joy.

De Profundis

B etter than Wordsworth himself I know what Wordsworth meant when he said –

'Suffering is permanent, obscure, and dark,
And has the nature of infinity.'

But while there were times when I rejoiced in the idea that my sufferings were to be endless, I could not bear them to be without meaning. Now I find hidden somewhere away in my nature something that tells me that nothing in the whole world is meaningless, and suffering least of all. That something hidden away in my nature, like a treasure in a field, is Humility.

De Profundis

Hélas!

To drift with every passion till my soul
Is a stringed lute on which all winds can play,
Is it for this that I have given away
Mine ancient wisdom, and austere control?
Methinks my life is a twice-written scroll
Scrawled over on some boyish holiday
With idle songs for pipe and virelay,
Which do but mar the secret of the whole.
Surely there was a time I might have trod
The sunlit heights, and from life's dissonance
Struck one clear chord to reach the ears of
God:
Is that time dead? lo! with a little rod
I did but touch the honey of romance –
And must I lose a soul's inheritance?